PEARSON LONGMAN

CORNERSTONE

1A

PEARSON English Learning System

Anna Uhl Chamot

Jim Cummins

Sharroky Hollie

PEARSON

Upper Saddle River, New Jersey • Boston, Massachusetts • Chandler, Arizona • Glenview, Illinois

Pearson Longman Cornerstone 1A

PEARSON English Learning System

Staff credits: The people who made up the Longman Cornerstone team, representing editorial, production, design, manufacturing, and marketing, are John Ade, Rhea Banker, Virginia Bernard, Daniel Comstock, David Dickey, Gina DiLlillo, Johnnie Farmer, Nancy Flaggman, Charles Green, Karen Kawaguchi, Ed Lamprich, Niki Lee, Jaime Leiber, Chris Leonowicz, Tara Maceyak, Linda Moser, Laurie Neaman, Leslie Patterson, Sherri Pemberton, Diane Pinkley, Liza Pleva, Susan Saslow, Chris Siley, Loretta Steeves, Kim Steiner, and Lauren Weidenman.

Text design and composition: The Quarasan Group, Inc.
Illustration and photo credits appear on page 186, which constitute an extension of this copyright page.

Library of Congress Cataloging-in-Publication Data
Chamot, Anna Uhl.
   Longman Cornerstone / Anna Uhl Chamot, Jim Cummins, Sharroky Hollie.
   p. cm. — (Longman Cornerstone)
   Includes index.
   1. Language arts (Elementary school)—United States. 2. Language arts (Elementary school)—Activity programs 3. English language—Study and teaching.
   I. Cummins, Jim II. Hollie, Sharroky III. Title.

ISBN-13: 978-0-3287-3348-4
ISBN-10: 0-3287-3348-2

Printed in the United States of America
9 17

About the Authors

Anna Uhl Chamot is a professor of secondary education and a faculty advisor for ESL in George Washington University's Department of Teacher Preparation. She has been a researcher and teacher trainer in content-based second-language learning and language-learning strategies. She co-designed and has written extensively about the Cognitive Academic Language Learning Approach (CALLA) and spent seven years implementing the CALLA model in the Arlington Public Schools in Virginia.

Jim Cummins is the Canada Research Chair in the Department of Curriculum, Teaching, and Learning of the Ontario Institute for Studies in Education at the University of Toronto. His research focuses on literacy development in multilingual school contexts, as well as on the potential roles of technology in promoting language and literacy development. His recent publications include: *The International Handbook of English Language Teaching* (co-edited with Chris Davison) and *Literacy, Technology, and Diversity: Teaching for Success in Changing Times* (with Kristin Brown and Dennis Sayers).

Sharroky Hollie is an assistant professor in teacher education at California State University, Dominguez Hills. His expertise is in the field of professional development, African-American education, and second-language methodology. He is an urban literacy visiting professor at Webster University, St. Louis. Sharroky is the Executive Director of the Center for Culturally Responsive Teaching and Learning (CCRTL) and the co-founding director of the nationally-acclaimed Culture and Language Academy of Success (CLAS).

Consultants and Reviewers

Rebecca Anselmo
Sunrise Acres Elementary School
Las Vegas, NV

Ana Applegate
Redlands School District
Redlands, CA

Terri Armstrong
Houston ISD
Houston, TX

Jacqueline Avritt
Riverside County Office of Ed.
Hemet, CA

Mitchell Bobrick
Palm Beach County School
West Palm Beach, FL

Victoria Brioso-Saldala
Broward County Schools
Fort Lauderdale, FL

Brenda Cabarga Schubert
Creekside Elementary School
Salinas, CA

Joshua Ezekiel
Bardin Elementary School
Salinas, CA

Veneshia Gonzalez
Seminole Elementary School
Okeechobee, FL

Carolyn Grigsby
San Francisco Unified School District
San Francisco, CA

Julie Grubbe
Plainfield Consolidated Schools
Chicago, IL

Yasmin Hernandez-Manno
Newark Public Schools
Newark, NJ

Janina Kusielewicz
Clifton Public Schools/Bilingual Ed.
& Basic Skills Instruction Dept.
Clifton, NJ

Mary Helen Lechuga
El Paso ISD
El Paso, TX

Gayle P. Malloy
Randolph School District
Randolph, MA

Randy Payne
Patterson/Taft Elementaries
Mesa, AZ

Marcie L. Schnegelberger
Alisal Union SD
Salinas, CA

Lorraine Smith
Collier County Schools
Naples, FL

Shawna Stoltenborg
Glendale Elementary School
Glen Burnie, MD

Denise Tiffany
West High School
Iowa City, IO

Dear Student,

Welcome to *Longman Cornerstone*!

We wrote *Longman Cornerstone* to help you learn to read, write, and speak English. We wrote a book that will make learning English and learning to read a lot of fun.

Cornerstone includes a mix of all subjects. We have written some make-believe stories and some true stories.

As you use this program, you will build on what you already know, learn new words and new information, and take part in projects. The projects will help you improve your English skills.

Learning a language takes time, but just like learning to swim or ride a two-wheeler, it is fun!

We hope you enjoy *Longman Cornerstone* as much as we enjoyed writing it for you!

Good luck!

Anna Uhl Chamot
Jim Cummins
Sharroky Hollie

Changes

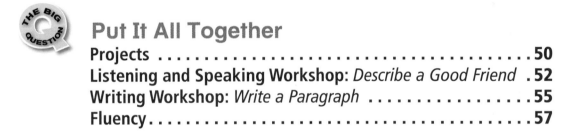

Contents

Communities

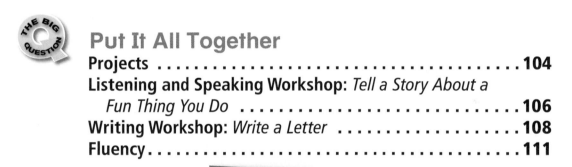

Traditions

Unit 1
Changes

Sometimes change is hard. But sometimes change is fun! Name some things that change. How do they change? Tell the class.

THE BIG Q QUESTION

How will you change this year as you meet new friends?

VIEW AND RESPOND

DVD *Watch the video. What is it about?*

Talk about the poster. What do you see?

Visit LongmanCornerstone.com.

What Do You Know about Changes?

Use what you know.

Children grow.

Flowers bloom.

4

Weather changes.

We make new friends.

Your Turn

Think about a change in your life.
Tell the class about it.

5

Sing about Changes

Changing Seasons

In fall, we rake the leaves.

In winter, we play in snow.

All throughout the year,

the seasons come and go.

Flowers grow in spring.

The summer breezes blow.

All throughout the year,

the seasons come and go.

Reading Tip

We read English from left to right and top to bottom.

Vocabulary

Words to Know

These words will help you understand the reading.

Sight Words

like

my

you

Story Words

new

backpack

1. I like my new book.

2. I give my book to you.

3. I have a new backpack.

Your Turn

Pick one word from either box.
Use the word in a sentence.
Ask your teacher for help.

Phonics

Short a; d, m, s

Listen for the sound at the beginning of the word. Say the sound.

a

d

m

s

WB   PH

4

Your Turn

Which letter stands for the sound at the beginning of the word?

a   d   m   d   m   s   a   d   m   a   m   s

9

Story Preview

Who is in the story?

Sam

mother

Sam

Where does the story happen?

home

school

Reading Strategy

Preview

Look at the pictures. What is the story about? As you read, see how previewing helps you understand the story.

I Am Sam

by Pamela Walker

illustrated by Kathryn Mitter

I am Sam.

I like my shoes.

I like my backpack.

I am sad.

I am new.

I am Sam.

I am Sam.

I am happy.

I love you.

Think It Over

Listen to the questions. Say the answers. Use Sight Words and Story Words.

1. Who does Sam meet at school?

2. Why is Sam sad?

3. How does Sam feel at the end of the story?

4. How do you make new friends?

83–84

Reading Strategy

Preview

How did previewing the story help you understand it?

Grammar and Writing

Rule

- Use **I am** + name or **I am** + adjective to talk about you.
- Use **not** to talk about things that are not true.
- Use **are you** to ask a person about himself or herself.

I am Ana.
I am happy.
I am not sad.

Reading Tip

Read the sentences in the boxes. If you don't understand the grammar rules, ask your teacher or a classmate for help.

I am = **I'm**

Are you Paco?

Yes, **I am**.

No, **I'm not**.
I'm Julio.

20

Practice

Example: <u>Are</u> you happy? Yes, I <u>am</u>.

1. I _____  at school.

2. I _____ not sad. I _____ happy.

3. _____ you Sam? Yes, I _____.

4. _____ you sad? No, I _____ not.

Apply

Example: A: Are you new?

B: Yes, I am.

Are you six?
Are you sad?
Are you happy?

Write!

Draw a picture of your face. Write about you.

I am Lee. I am new.
I am happy.

Vocabulary

 Audio

Words to Know

These words will help you understand the reading.

1. I see a dog.

2. The dog is little.

Sight Words

see

is

little

3. I see a butterfly.

Story Words

butterfly

frog

4. Can you see the frog?

 WB
9

22

Your Turn

Pick one word from either box.

Use the word in a sentence.

Phonics

Short e; f, l, t

Listen for the sound at the beginning of the word. Say the sound.

 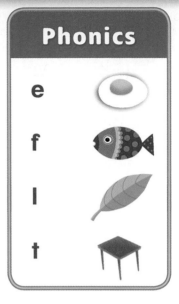
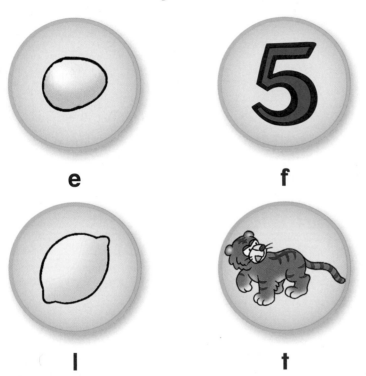

e

f

l

t

WB PH
10

Your Turn

Which letter stands for the sound at the beginning of the word?

f l t   e f l   e l t   e f t

23

Story Preview

Who is in the story?

caterpillar

frog

Where does the story happen?

tree

pond

Reading Strategy

Sequence

Sequence tells when things happen in order. What is the sequence of this story?

As you read, see how things happen in order.

I Met Ted

by Christian Foley
illustrated by Don Tate

25

I am a caterpillar.
I am little.

I met Ted.

Ted is a tadpole.

See Ted.

Ted is a fat tadpole.

He is a fat, fat tadpole.

Ted is big.

Ted sits and sits.

 I am at home.

Ted is a frog.

I am a butterfly.

Think It Over

Audio

Listen to the questions. Say the answers. Use Sight Words and Story Words.

1. How big is the tadpole at first?

2. How does the tadpole change?

3. How do the caterpillar and the tadpole change?

4. How do animals change?

Speaking Tip

Look at the pictures again. Retell the story. This will help you learn new words.

11–12

Reading Strategy

Sequence

How did thinking about sequence help you understand the story?

Frogs

1 A frog begins as an egg. ▶

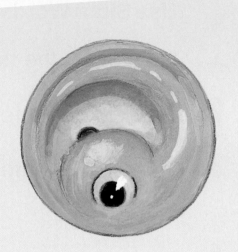

◀**2** It is now a tadpole.

3 Back legs grow. ▶

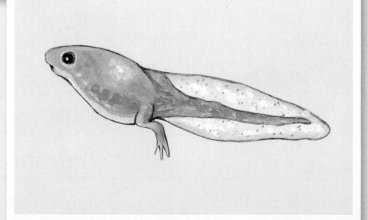

4 Front legs grow. ▶

▲

5 It is now a frog.

Activity to Do

Draw pictures to show change.

- Draw a tadpole.
- Draw a frog.
- Talk about your pictures.

35

Grammar and Writing

Rule

- Use the pronoun *he* for a boy or man, *she* for a girl or woman, and *it* for a thing.
- Use the verb *is* with *he*, *she*, and *it*.
- To ask a question, use *is* before *he*, *she*, or *it*.

She is a girl.

He is a boy.
He is not a girl.

He is = **he's**   It is = **It's**
She is = **she's**   is not = **isn't**

It's a backpack.

Is he six?
No, **he isn't**.

Practice

Example: <u>Is</u> Ted a frog? Yes, <u>he is</u>.

1. _____ Ms. Cho a teacher? Yes, _____.

2. _____ Carla five? No, _____ not.

3. _____ the book new? Yes, _____.

4. _____ Ted a butterfly? No, _____ not.

5. _____ the bag little? No, _____ not.

Apply

Example: A: Is he seven?

B: No, he isn't. He's six.

Is she new?
Is he happy?
Is she six?

Write!

Draw a picture of a classmate.
Write about your classmate.

She is Lucy. She is six.
She is happy.

Vocabulary

Words to Know

These words
will help you
understand
the reading.

1. Do you have
   a snack for me?

Sight Words

have

me

too

2. My hat is
   too big.

Story Words

three

fun

3. Three pals have fun.

Your Turn

Pick one word from either box.

Use the word in a sentence.

Phonics

Short i; n, p

Listen for the sound at the beginning of the word. Say the sound.

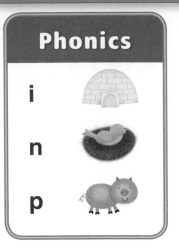

Phonics

i

n

p

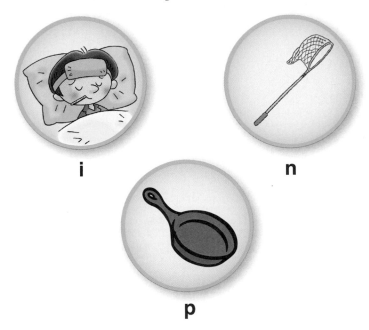

i

n

p

WB   PH

16

Your Turn

Which letter stands for the sound at the beginning of the word?

 i n p

i n p

i n p

i n p

Story Preview

Who is in the story?

Tip   Kim   Don   pals

Where does the story happen?

city   country

Reading Strategy

Compare and Contrast

In the story, what is the same? What is different? As you read, see how things are alike and different.

Shared Reading Your teacher will show you how to use the strategy. Listen, watch, and practice.

Tip

by Katrinka Moore

illustrated by Mary Roja

I am Tip.

I am sad.

Kim is sad, too.

Kim is a pal.

I can see Kim.

I can sit in Don's van.

I have three new pals.

Ann, Ed, and Mel pet me.

I am not too sad.

I can have fun.

Think It Over

Audio

Listen to the questions. Say the answers. Use Sight Words and Story Words.

1. Who is Kim?

2. Why is Tip sad?

3. What is Tip's new home like?

4. How do you feel in a new home?

Speaking Tip

Practice asking for information. Ask a partner a question about the story. Use Sight and Story Words.

WB

17–18

Reading Strategy

Compare and Contrast

How did comparing and contrasting parts of the story help you understand it?

Grammar and Writing

Rule

- The pronoun **we** is for you and other people. **They** is for two or more people, places, or things.
- Use **are** with *we* and *they*.
- To ask a question, use **are** before *we* or *they*.

We are at school. **We are not** at home.

We are = **We're**   They are = **They're**
are not = **aren't**

Are they computers?

Yes, **they are.**

Example: <u>Is</u> the school big? Yes, it <u>is</u>.

1. _____ they pals? Yes, they _____.

2. _____ Don a student? Yes, he _____.

3. _____ the class fun? Yes, it _____.

4. _____ they books? No, they _____ not.

Apply

Example: A: Are we in class?

B: Yes, we are.

Are they pals?
Are they students?
Is she a teacher?

Write!

Draw a picture of your class. Write about your class.

We are in class.
Ms. Lopez is my teacher.
Lee and Jin are students.
They are my pals.

WB
19–20

Your teacher will help you choose one of these projects.

Written

Write about a new friend.

Write a story to tell about a new friend.

THE BIG QUESTION

How will you change this year as you meet new friends? Talk about it.

Oral	**Visual/Active**
Introduce a new friend.	**Draw a new friend.**
Introduce a new friend to your class.	Draw pictures to show what your new friend looks like.

Describe a Good Friend

Tell the class about a good friend.

1 Prepare

Think about a good friend. Draw a picture of him or her. Write four sentences to describe your friend.

1. Jenna is my friend.
2. She has black hair.
3. She has brown eyes.
4. She is fun.

2 Practice and Present

Show the picture of your friend to the class. Use the sentences you wrote. Describe your friend to the class.

As you speak, do this:

- Say each word clearly.
- Say your sentences slowly.
- Use the same sentence type as the examples.

As you listen, do this:

- Look at the picture.
- Listen for words that describe the picture.
- How do the picture and the words help you understand what people say?
- If you don't understand, ask questions.

Listening Tip

Listen to your teacher. Learn the expression, my best friend. Who is your best friend?

❸ Evaluate

Ask yourself these questions:

- Did you describe your friend well?
- You listened for words. How did that help you understand what people said?

Writing Workshop

Write a Paragraph

You will write a paragraph. A paragraph is a group of sentences about something.

I am Min. I am six. My sister is Lian. She's four. My dad is Deshi. He is fun. My mom is Jia. She is nice. I love my family.

❶ Prewrite List the people in your family in a chart. Tell something about each person.

Carlos listed his ideas in this chart.

Person	Name	Something about him/her
me	Carlos	six
mother	Luz	smart
father	Oscar	brave

2 **Draft** Write a paragraph. Use the ideas in your chart. Use new words from the unit.

3 **Revise** Read your paragraph. Use the Revising Checklist to make your writing better.

Here is Carlos's paragraph.

I am Carlos. I am six. My mother is Luz. She's smart. My father is Oscar. He's brave. We are a happy family.

4 Edit Trade papers. Correct your partner's paragraph. Use the Checklist.

5 Publish Make a clean copy of your paragraph. Share it with the class.

Editing Checklist

✓ Each sentence starts with a capital.

✓ Each sentence ends with a period.

✓ Contractions are correct (*he's, isn't*).

For Each Reading...

1. Listen to the sentences.

2. Listen and use your finger to follow the words.

3. Listen, use your finger, and say the words.

Sam has a new school.

I Am Sam

Ted is a fat tadpole.

I Met Ted

Tip has three new pals.

Tip

WB

25–26

Unit 2
Communities

Some communities are big. Some communities are small. We all live in a community.

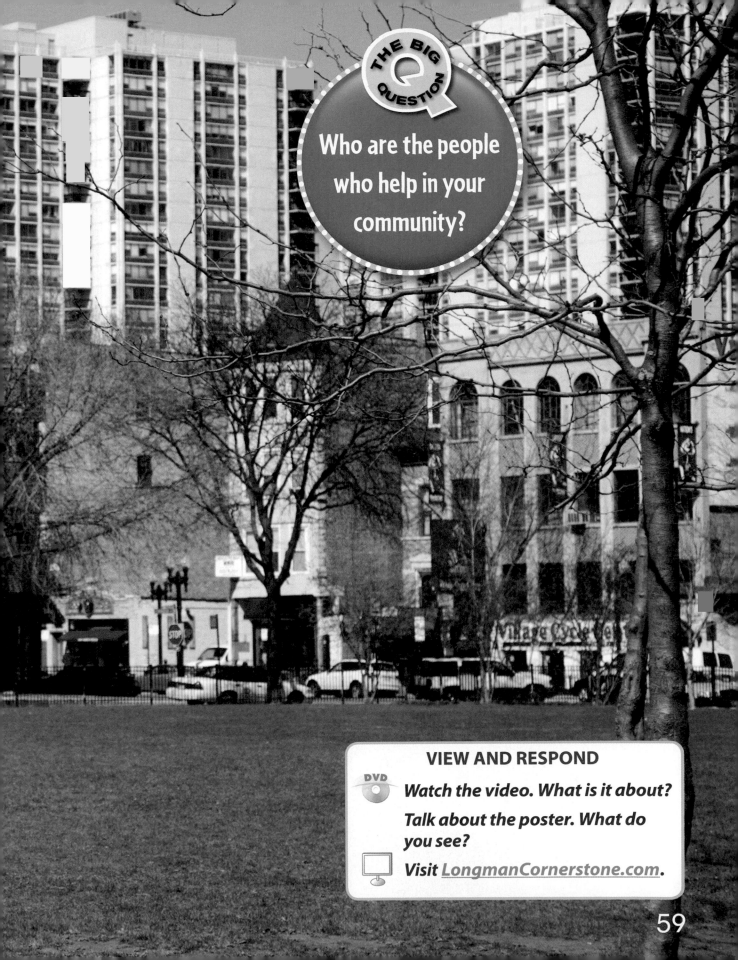

THE BIG QUESTION

Who are the people who help in your community?

VIEW AND RESPOND

Watch the video. What is it about?

Talk about the poster. What do you see?

Visit LongmanCornerstone.com.

What Do You Know about Communities?

Use what you know.

A city is a community.

A bus driver works in a community.

A small town is a community.

A teacher works in a community.

People live and work in a community.

Your Turn

Think about a place in your community. Tell the class about it.

Sing about Communities

People in the Community

The people on the street say,

"Hello, hello, hello."

"Hello, hello, hello."

"Hello, hello, hello."

The people on the street say,

"Hello, hello, hello,"

all over town.

The driver on the bus says,

"Hello, hello, hello."

"Hello, hello, hello."

"Hello, hello, hello."

The driver on the bus says,

"Hello, hello, hello,"

all over town.

Reading Tip

We read English from left to right and top to bottom.

These words will help you understand the reading.

Sight Words

he

she

about

Story Words

people

letter

Vocabulary Audio

Words to Know

1. Rosa asks for help.

2. He can help.

3. She asks about his important job.

4. People can mail a letter.

Your Turn

Pick a word from either box.

Use the word in a sentence.

Phonics

Short o; c, h

Look at each picture and word.
Listen to the letter sounds.
Say the word.

hot

doll

on

cat

 WB PH

30

Your Turn

Sound out the words. Point to the word for the picture.

dog   dig   hit   fit   pot   pat   hot   cot

Story Preview

Who is in this story?

people

Where does the story happen?

community

Reading Strategy

Prior Knowledge

Use what you know to help you read. As you read, see how prior knowledge helps you understand.

Shared Reading Your teacher will show you how to use the strategy. Listen, watch, and practice.

66

People Can Help

by Lawrence Po

illustrated by Apryl Stott and Sue Miller

Dot can help Ned send a letter.

Sal can help Mom and Tam.

She can take Mom and Tam

on the bus.

Ed can sit at a desk.

He can help get a book
about a cat.

Dan is sad about his
dog, Top.

Nan can help Top.

Tom can help Tim, Pam,
and Ted cross.
A lot of people can help.

Think It Over

Audio

Listen to the questions. Say the answers.
Use Sight Words and Story Words.

1. What does Ned give Dot?

2. How does Sal help Mom and Tam?

3. Why is Dan sad?

4. Why do people help?

WB
31–32

Reading Strategy

Prior Knowledge

How did using what you know help you read?

Grammar and Writing

Rule

- Use **can** + verb to talk about things people are able to do.
- Use **can** + **not** + verb for things people are not able to do.
- To ask a question, use **can** + subject + verb.

I **can** play soccer.

Reading Tip

Read the sentences in the boxes. If you don't understand the grammar rules, ask your teacher or a classmate for help.

cannot = **can't**

Can he skateboard?
Yes, he **can**.

He **can't** swim.

76

Practice

Example: <u>Can</u> you run? Yes, I <u>can</u>.

1. ___ you swim? Yes, I ___.

2. ___ he skate? No, he ___ .

3. ___ she sing? No, she ___.

4. ___ they ski? Yes, they ___.

Apply

Example: A: Can you
             play soccer?

         B: Yes, I can.

| Can you swim? |
| Can you run? |
| Can you skate? |

Write!

Draw a picture of things you can do.
Write about them.

I can swim. I can play
soccer. I can skateboard.

WB

33–34

Vocabulary

Words to Know

These words will help you understand the reading.

1. Look at the man in back.

2. He passes to another man.

Sight Words

look

the

another

3. This glass of milk is a delicious snack.

Story Words

delicious

snack

Your Turn

Pick a word from either box.

Use the word in a sentence.

Ask your teacher for help.

35

78

Phonics

Short u; b, j

Look at each picture and word.
Listen to the letter sounds.
Say the word.

 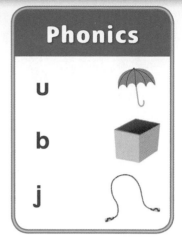

jam

bus

up

hug

36

Your Turn

Which letter stands for the missing sound?

__ u g

c __ p

__ e d

b __ g

Story Preview

Who is in the story?

Bud

Dad

Pat

Where does the story happen?

shops

Reading Strategy

Main Idea

What is the most important idea in the story? It is the main idea. As you read, look for the main idea.

Bud and His Dad

by Denise Lewis

illustrated by Barbara Spurll

Bud and his dad can

hop to the shop.

Bud can have milk and
jam. Bud likes milk and jam
a lot. Mmmm.

Bud and his dad hop to another shop.

Bud and his dad see Pat.

Bud can have another snack.

Mmmm. Mmmm.

Look! A blue snack is on Bud.
Mmmm, it is delicious!

Think It Over

Audio **Listen to the questions. Say the answers. Use Sight Words and Story Words.**

1. Where do Bud and his dad hop?

2. How can Bud and his dad hop?

3. Why does Bud like milk and jam?

4. Why are shops important?

Speaking Tip

Look at the pictures again. Retell the story. This will help you learn new words.

37–38

Reading Strategy

Main Idea

How did understanding the main idea help you read?

Grammar and Writing

Rule

- The possessive adjectives **my, your, her, his, their,** and **our** show who owns something.
- You can also use: name + apostrophe (') + **s**.

I'm Dan. This is **my** mom and sister. This is **our** cat.

I	→	my
he	→	his
she	→	her
it	→	its
we	→	our
they	→	their

Chang has a ball. This is **his** ball.

This is **Maria's** kite.

88

Example: (Anna) That is <u>Anna's</u> dog.

1. (he) This is ___ dad.

2. (I) That is ___ backpack.

3. (Julio) This is ___ book.

4. (they) This is ___ pencil.

Apply

Is that your paper?
Is that your pen?
Is that your pencil?

Example: A: Is that your book?

B: No, it isn't. It's Jin's book.

Write!

Draw a picture of something that belongs to a friend. Write about it.

This is Jed. This is Jed's bike. His bike is new. It is red.

WB
39–40

89

Vocabulary

Words to Know

1. I can use this pen.

2. School can be fun.

3. The doctor got mail today.

These words will help you understand the reading.

Sight Words

use

this

be

Story Words

doctor

mail

Your Turn

Pick a word from either box.

Use the word in a sentence.

41

Phonics

Long a; r, w

Look at each picture and word.
Listen to the letter sounds.
Say the word.

 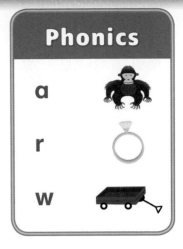

plate

flame

wet

run

WB PH

42

Your Turn

Sound out the words. Point to the word for the picture.

wade   made

take   rake

gate   get

91

Story Preview

What is the story about?

The story is about Jane.
Jane brings mail to people.

Reading Strategy

Sequence

Sequence tells when things happen in order. What is the sequence of this story? As you read, put the events in order to help you understand the story.

Jane Has a Job

by Cecelia Rice

illustrated by Sue Miller

Jane has a job.

The mail will not be late.

Jane will put this
letter in a red slot.

Jane can hand mail
to Doctor Ron. Doctor
Ron helps pets get well.

Doctor Ron can use
this mail. It will help sick
cats and dogs get well.

Jane has a letter for Rob.

His pal Wes Wade sent it.

Jane can help a lot of people.

Think It Over

Listen to the questions. Say the answers. Use Sight Words and Story Words.

1. What does Jane bring to people?

2. What kind of job does Jane have?

3. How did Jane help Doctor Ron?

4. Why is it important for us to get mail?

WB
43–44

Reading Strategy

Sequence

How did thinking about sequence help you understand the story?

Mailing a Letter

1 Nate can mail a letter. ▶

2 ◀ Jill can load it in the truck.

3 The letter gets sorted. ▶

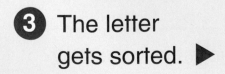

4 Bill will deliver the letter. ▶

5 ▲ Nat will get the letter from Nate.

Activity to Do

You can become a mail carrier.

- Write a letter.
- Tell something about your community.
- Deliver your letter to a friend.

101

Grammar and Writing

Rule

- Use **will** + verb to talk about things you or other people are going to do in the future.
- Use **will not** for things you are not going to do.
- To ask a question, Use **will** + subject + verb.

My dog **will get** the paper.
He will not get the mail.

will not = **won't**

Will you **call** your friend tonight?

No, I won't.
He will call me!

102

Example: <u>Will</u> you get the mail? Yes, I <u>will</u>.

1. ___ he go to the park? No, he ___.

2. ___ she do her homework? Yes, she ___.

3. ___ you watch a movie? Yes, I ___.

4. ___ you eat the snack? No, I ___.

Apply

Example: A: Will you see a
                    friend today?

               B: Yes, I will.

| do homework |
| go to the park |
| watch a movie |

Write!

Draw a picture of three things you will do this weekend. Write about them.

I will watch a movie.
I will go to the park.
I will play soccer.

WB
45–46

103

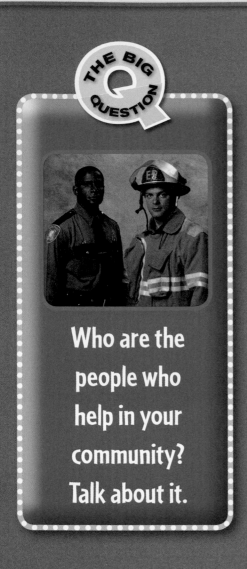

Who are the people who help in your community? Talk about it.

Your teacher will help you choose one of these projects.

Written

Write about a person in your community.

What does the person do? What job does the person have? Write about it.

Oral

 ## Visual/Active

Interview a person in your community.

Talk to a person in your community who has an interesting job. What makes the job interesting?

When I grow up...

What job in your community would you like to have? Act out how you would do that job.

47–48

Listening and Speaking Workshop

Tell a Story About a Fun Thing You Do

Tell the class a story about a fun thing you do.

1 Prepare

Tell a story about what you do for fun. Write four sentences about it.

2 Practice and Present

Practice with a partner. Then tell your story to the class.

1. It's fun to climb hills!
2. I can climb the big hill in the park.
3. I climb the hill after school.
4. It's fun because I can see everyone.

As you speak, do this:

- Use your voice, hands, and facial expressions to tell story.

- Show your feelings. Say a sentence that ends with a *!*.

As you listen, do this:

- Look at the speaker. Ask questions if you don't understand.

- Listen for words you learned. How does this help you understand what people say?

- Think about what you learn from people's words, faces, and hands. How can you get clues about hidden ideas or information?

③ Evaluate

Ask yourself these questions:

- How well did you understand the directions?

- How did you use your voice, hands, and face to tell the story?

> **Listening Tip**
>
> Listen to your teacher. Learn the expression, *have fun*. How do you have fun?

> **Speaking Tip**
>
> Speak in short and long sentences. Use words like *and, but,* or *because.*

Writing Workshop

Write a Letter

You will write a letter to a friend.

1. **Prewrite** List the things you will do after school. Look at Ho's list.

> October 3
>
> Dear Chang,
>
>   Today I will:
>
> 1. look for my ball and bat
> 2. go to the park
> 3. play baseball with Peter
> 4. eat ice cream
>
>   Your friend,
>   Ho

2. **Draft** Write a letter. Use the ideas in your list. Use new words from the unit.

3. Revise Read your letter. Use the Revising Checklist to make your writing better.

December 10
Dear Chang,
How are you? After school I will get my ~~basball~~ *baseball* and bat. Then I will go to the park with my ~~frend~~ *friend* Peter. We will play baseball. Then we will eat ice cream at his house.
Your friend,
Ho

Revising Checklist
✓ Do I tell the date?
✓ Do I write the person's name on the letter?
✓ Do I include details about my plans?

4. **Edit** Trade papers. Correct your partner's letter. Use the Editing Checklist.

5. **Publish** Make a clean copy of your letter. Share it with the class.

Editing Checklist

✓ Each sentence starts with a capital.

✓ Each sentence ends with a period.

✓ Possessive words are correct (*my, Anna's*).

Spelling Tip

You learned the long a sound before. When the word or syllable ends in *e*, the a sound is long.

pl**a**t̄e

b**a**s̄eball

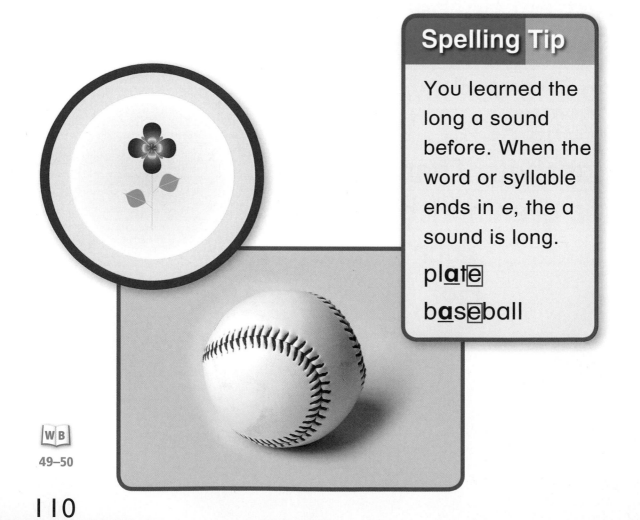

For Each Reading . . .

1. Listen to the sentences.

2. Listen and use your finger to follow the words.

3. Listen, use your finger, and say the words.

Sal can help Mom and Tam.

People Can Help

Bud can have milk and jam.

Bud and His Dad

Jane can hand mail to
Doctor Ron.

Jane Has a Job

WB
51–52

Unit 3
Traditions

People celebrate traditions. Thanksgiving is a tradition. Tell the class about a tradition in your family.

THE BIG QUESTION

What is your favorite way to celebrate?

VIEW AND RESPOND

Watch the video. What is it about?

Talk about the poster. What do you see?

Visit LongmanCornerstone.com.

113

What Do You Know about Traditions? Audio

Use what you know.

People follow traditions.

A Thanksgiving parade is a tradition.

On Valentine's Day, people give cards to each other.

On the Fourth of July, families have picnics.

Your Turn

Think about your favorite tradition. Tell the class about it.

Sing about Traditions

Family Traditions Song

Family, family, get together.

Time to celebrate, all together.

Some have Christmas.

Some have Kwanzaa.

Some have Hanukkah.

Some have Ramadan.

Family, family, get together.

Time to celebrate, all together.

We will eat.

What will you bring?

Gather round

And let us sing.

Family, family, get together.

Time to celebrate, all together.

Vocabulary

Audio

Words to Know

1. Lots of people play at birthday parties.

2. I like to play, too.

3. I like green balloons best.

4. A carnival is a celebration.

5. People can wear a costume.

These words will help you understand the reading.

Sight Words

of

to

green

Story Words

carnival

celebration

costume

Your Turn

Pick one word from either box.

Use the word in a sentence.

Ask your teacher for help.

55

Phonics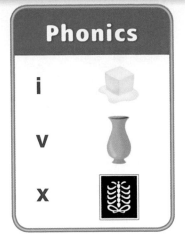

Long i; v, x

Look at each picture and word.
Listen to the letter sounds.
Say the word.

van

ox

five

ride

WB   PH

56

Your Turn

Which letter stands for the sound in the middle of the word?

b __ ke   w __ ve   b __ x   k __ te

119

Story Preview

What is the story about?.

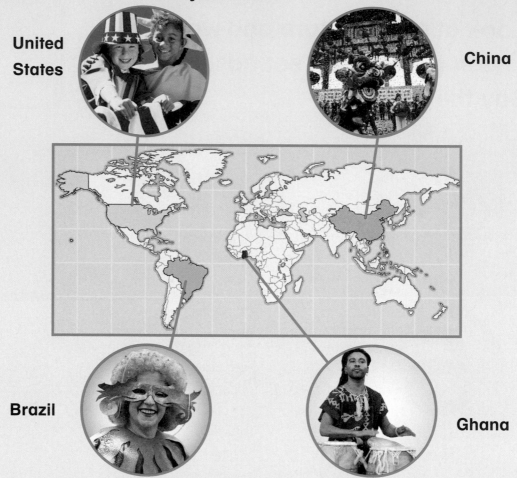

United States

China

Brazil

Ghana

The story is about celebrations around the world.

Reading Strategy

Compare and Contrast

Compare means to see how things are alike. Contrast means to see how things are different. As you read, see how things are alike and different.

Celebration Time!

by Carol Johnson

I am having lots and lots of fun!
It is celebration time!

It's the New Year. It can be
named for an ox, rat, pig, or ram.
Around the world, it is
celebration time!

I can have a fun time at
a carnival.
I can put on a big blue wig
and a mask to hide.

I can smile and dress up.
I can dress up in a red
and green costume.
It is fun to dress up in a hat.

On July 4, I can dress up
in red, white, and blue.
I can wave a flag.

Mom, Dad, and I are gazing at the sky.
Pop! Pop! Pop! Pop! Pop! Pop!

In Ghana, tribes plant crops.
It is celebration time.
Lots of drums go tap, tap, tap!

Think It Over

Audio **Listen to the questions. Say the answers. Use Sight Words and Story Words.**

1. What can the New Year be named for?

2. Why do people like to dress up for celebrations?

3. Compare how people celebrate.

4. How does your family have celebrations?

WB
57–58

Reading Strategy

Compare and Contrast

How did comparing and contrasting help you understand the story?

Celebrations

China

In China, people dress in dragon costumes to celebrate the New Year. ▶

Brazil

▲ In Brazil, people celebrate Carnival with feasts and parades for days and days.

United States

In the United States, people celebrate Independence Day with fireworks. ▶

Ghana

▲ In Ghana, Djembe drummers perform at celebrations.

Activity to Do

On Flag Day we celebrate our flag.

- Draw and color a U.S. flag.
- Write a story about your flag.
- Show your drawing. Tell your story to the class.

131

Grammar and Writing

Rule

- Use verbs with **-ing** to talk about things you are doing right now.
- Use **am**, **is**, or **are** before the verb.
- To make a question, you can start with **What is**, **are**, or **am**, and then the subject and verb.

She **is swinging.**

Reading Tip

Read the sentences in the boxes. If you don't understand the grammar rules, ask your teacher or a classmate for help.

What is he **doing?**

He**'s drawing.**

What are they **doing?**

They **are playing** baseball.

Practice

Example: I <u>am</u> call<u>ing</u> my pal.

1. He ____ kick ____ the ball.

2. We ____ play ____ baseball.

3. The girls ____ listen ____ to music.

4. They ____ throw ____ the ball.

Apply

**Pretend to do an activity.
Your partner guesses.**

> play basketball
> ride a bicycle
> swim

Example: A: What am I doing?

   B: You're jumping rope!

Write!

**Draw a picture of you doing your favorite
activity. Write about your picture.**

I'm playing baseball.
I am throwing the ball.
My friend is catching the ball.

WB
59–60

Vocabulary

Words to Know

These words will help you understand the reading.

1. They go on a ride **first**.

2. **Then** they will play **with** friends.

3. The **Thanksgiving** **parade** is fun.

4. They go on a **sleigh**.

Sight Words

first

then

with

Story Words

Thanksgiving

parade

sleigh

Your Turn

Pick one word from either box.
Use the word in a sentence.

61

Phonics

Long u; k, ck

Look at each picture and word.
Listen to the letter sounds.
Say the word.

 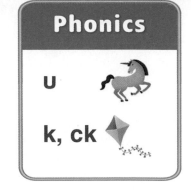

kite

duck

cube

WB PH

62

Your Turn

Sound out the words. Point to the word for the picture.

use   us   up

kit   kick   kite

sock   sob   spot

135

Story Preview

What is the story about?

**The story is about Thanksgiving.
Thanksgiving is a celebration.**

Reading Strategy

Summarize

What is the most important information in a story or poem? Say or write about it in your own words. As you read, identify important information.

Reading Tip

Take notes as you read.

Thanksgiving Time!

by Mary O'Donnell

At Thanksgiving time we used
cups and plates.
First we sat and then we ate.

People came to a new land to
make a good home.

June helps with Jules and Gram.

Zack hands Pam a plate of yams.

A big parade will pass us by.
I gaze at a big star up in the sky.

Then I see big pipes and a drum.
I sing a tune and I hum and hum.

I am glad Ken and June came.

It is fun to see a big
Thanksgiving game.

Thanksgiving time ends with
a fun sleigh ride.
I hum a tune while my family
and pals sit by my side.

Think It Over

Audio
Listen to the questions. Say the answers. Use Sight Words and Story Words.

1. What does Zack pass to Pam?

2. How does June help Gram?

3. Why do people like to celebrate Thanksgiving?

4. What is the most important part of Thanksgiving?

63–64

Reading Strategy

Summarize

How did summarizing the story help you to understand it?

Grammar and Writing

Rule

- An adjective describes a noun or a pronoun.
- An adjective can come before a noun. It can also come after *is*, *am*, or *are*.
- To ask questions about colors, you can say *What color is it?* or *What colors are they?*

His shirt is **green** and **white**.

He has **brown** hair. It is **curly**.

The boy is **happy**.

What color **is** her shirt?

What color are her eyes?

It is **red** and **white**.

They are **brown**.

Example: My $\underset{\text{N}}{\underline{\text{hair}}}$ is $\underset{\text{A}}{\underline{\text{brown}}}$.

1. I'm a <u>girl</u>. I have <u>green</u> eyes.

2. He is <u>tall</u>. He is not <u>short</u>.

3. The <u>boy</u> has a <u>white</u> shirt.

4. My <u>hair</u> is not <u>long</u>. It's <u>short</u>.

Ask questions with *What color is* or *What color are*.

book	bookbag
hair	pants

Example: A: What color are your eyes?

   B: They're brown.

Write!

Draw a picture of you. Describe yourself.

I have green eyes.
My hair is brown. It is long.

Vocabulary

Audio

Words to Know

These words will help you understand the reading.

1. We have a red, white, and blue flag in our school.

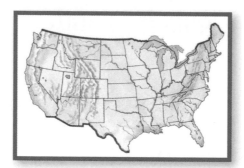

2. We live in North America.

3. The moon is full.

4. We learn about the moon at school.

Sight Words

white
blue
our

Story Words

America
moon
school

Your Turn

Pick one word from either box.
Use the word in a sentence.

Phonics

Long o; g, z

Look at each picture and word.
Listen to the letter sounds.
Say the word.

 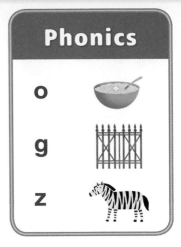

gate

zip

stove

hole

WB   PH

68

Your Turn

Which letter stands for the sound in the beginning of the word?

g n z   g c z   o g z   o t g

151

Story Preview

What is the story about?

The story is about the American flag.

Reading Strategy

Context Clues

Context clues tell you about words. Use context clues to understand new words. As you read, see how context clues help you understand words.

A Flag

by Bonnie Lee

In America a flag is red, white,
and blue! America is our home.

I can see red and white
and blue. It is our flag.

I can see lots of flags.
Flags stand in my school, and
they stand at my home.

I can see lots of colorful
flags at games.
A man is glad to stand
with a flag at a game.

A man lands on the moon,
and he is glad to wear a
flag on his arm.

The flag is on a flagpole.
The man pokes a hole to
make the flag stand up.

I am at home and feel safe
with America's flag. I gaze at
it, and I see a beautiful flag!

Think It Over

Audio

Listen to the questions. Say the answers. Use Sight Words and Story Words.

1. What colors make up the flag in America?

2. Why do people wave our flag?

3. Why did the man poke a hole in the moon?

4. How does seeing our flag make you feel?

WB 69–70

Reading Strategy

Context Clues

How did using context clues help you understand new words?

Grammar and Writing

Rule

- Use the **simple present** for things that happen again and again or that are always true.
- For **he, she,** or **it,** add **-s** after the verb.
- To make a negative sentence, use **do** or **does** + **not**.

She **makes** sandcastles.

In the summer, I **play** on the beach.

does not = **doesn't**
do not = **don't**

She **doesn't get** up early.

Example: (starts) School <u>starts</u> at 8:00.

1. (get up) He ___ early every day.

2. (sit) They ___ by the pool.

3. (sleep) She ___ late on Saturday.

4. (take) He ___ his dog to the park.

Apply

Talk about things you do in the summer.

Example: A: In the summer, I skate.

   B: I do, too. / I don't skate.

Write!

Draw a picture of things you do in the summer. Describe them.

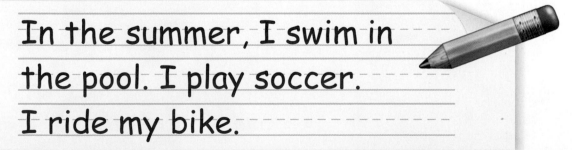

In the summer, I swim in the pool. I play soccer. I ride my bike.

WB
72–73

Projects

Your teacher will help you choose one of these projects.

Written

Write about a family celebration.

What do you do? Who is there? Write about it.

THE BIG QUESTION

What is your favorite way to celebrate? Talk about it.

Oral	Visual/Active
Describe a family celebration.	**Draw a picture of a family celebration.**
Without saying what the celebration is, describe it. Can your class guess what your family celebration is?	Draw a picture that shows your family celebrating.

Listening and Speaking Workshop

Description Guessing Game

Play this game to practice describing animals.

1 **Prepare** G.O. 117

Choose three animals. Draw a picture of each animal. For each animal, write words in a word web. See the word web for the word bird.

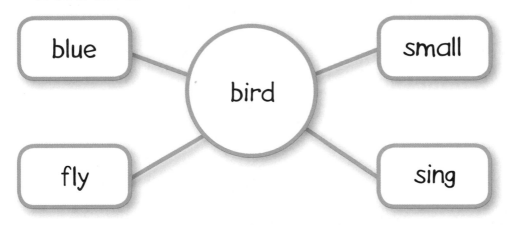

2 **Practice and Present**

Don't let your classmates see your pictures. When it's your turn, use your words to describe an animal. Who can guess what the animal is? When someone guesses correctly, hold up your picture. Then the winner takes a turn.

As you speak, do this:

- Use short and long sentences.
- Have fun. Remember, this is a game.

As you listen, do this:

- Take notes in your notebook.
- Listen for words you know.
- If an idea or information is not clear, listen for clues. Think again.
- Think about what you know about birds.

3 Evaluate

- Did you choose good words to describe?
- How well did you understand the rules?

More Practice

Choose a picture of an animal you don't know.
Your partner listens as you describe it.

- Don't show the picture.
- Tell the most important thing and two details about the animal.
- Ask your partner to guess what it is.
- Your partner can repeat the same steps with you.

Writing Workshop

Write a Descriptive Paragraph

A descriptive paragraph tells about a person or place.

1 **Prewrite** First , think about a place you like.
How does it look? How does it feel? What do
you do there? Then draw a web and write in it.

Ana wrote in her web.

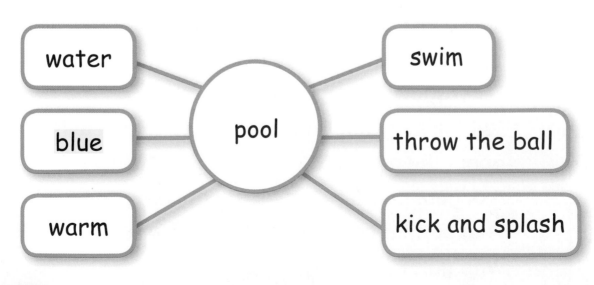

2 **Draft** Write a descriptive paragraph. Use the ideas in your web. Use new words from the unit.

3 **Revise** Read your paragraph. Use the Revising Checklist to make it better.

Here is Ana's descriptive paragraph.

I like the pool. The pool is big and the water is ~~blu~~ blue and warm. My sister and I swim in the water. We throw the ~~bal~~ ball and kick and splash.

Revising Checklist

✓ Do I use adjectives to describe things?

✓ Do I describe how the place looks?

✓ Do I tell what I do in this place?

4 **Edit** Trade papers. Correct your partner's paragraph. Use the Editing Checklist.

5 **Publish** Make a clean copy of your paragraph. Share it with the class.

Spelling Tip

When a short word ends in *l*, *f*, or *s*, you often double the last letters: ball, puff, less.

Editing Checklist

✓ The subjects and verbs agree.

✓ Pronouns agree with verbs.

✓ Verb tenses are correct.

For Each Reading . . .

1. Listen to the sentences.

2. Listen and use your finger to follow the words.

3. Listen, use your finger, and say the words.

I can have lots and lots of fun!

Celebration Time

First we sat and then we ate and ate and ate.

Thanksgiving Time

Our flag is red and white and blue.

A Flag

77–78

A

about

Tim asks a question **about** math.

after

He took the pumpkin home **after** he picked it.

again

I visit my family **again**.

all

We **all** worked in the garden.

America

We live in **America**.

Animals

Animals are helpful.

another

Here comes **another** friend.

B

baby

This is a **baby**.

backpack

I wear my **backpack** to school.

ball

I play with my **ball**.

be

Getting mail can **be** fun.

because

Ducks swim **because** they live in water.

before

Kim hugged Tip **before** he left.

best

Andrew always wins this game. He's the **best** player.

big

I like to play with my **big** brother.

birds

Birds eat seeds on the ground.

blossom

It is a pretty **blossom**.

blue

The water is **blue**.

A
B
C
D
E
F
G
H
I
J
K
L
M
N
O
P
Q
R
S
T
U
V
W
X
Y
Z

A
B
C
D
E
F
G
H
I
J
K
L
M
N
O
P
Q
R
S
T
U
V
W
X
Y
Z

bought

He **bought** a snack.

build

My dad is helping me **build** a kite.

butterfly

A **butterfly** has big wings.

C

carnival

We go to the **carnival**.

cattle

The **cattle** are
in a field.

celebration

A **celebration** is
a special time.

cello

My cousin Sam plays the **cello**
really well.

come

He will **come** to take
Jimmy's letter.

costume

We wear a
costume.

174

D

delicious

Chicken is a **delicious** food.

different

Owen and Mzee are **different** animals.

doctor

The **doctor** helps me get well.

duckling

The **duckling** is small.

E

eat

Some people like to **eat** with chopsticks.

enjoy

I really **enjoy** reading.

F

feathers

Birds have **feathers**.

first

Dad cut the turkey **first**.

A
B
C
D
E
F
G
H
I
J
K
L
M
N
O
P
Q
R
S
T
U
V
W
X
Y
Z

A B C D E F G H I J K L M N O P Q R S T U V W X Y Z

food chain

Plants and animals are part of the **food chain**.

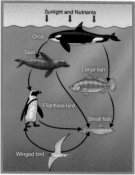

friend

He is my **friend**.

frog

A **frog** jumps and swims.

from

Joe takes a soccer ball **from** his bag.

fun

A party is **fun**.

G

green

This balloon is **green**.

grow

We water the plants so they will **grow**.

H

have

They **have** a ball.

he

He helps Tracey cross the street.

hippopotamus

A **hippopotamus** is a big animal.

horses

Horses pull the cart.

I

is

Ted **is** fat.

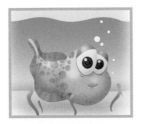

K

know

I **know** how to sew.

L

letter

Jim writes a **letter** to send to José.

like

I **like** bedtime.

little

The dog is **little**.

live

I **live** in a busy city.

A
B
C
D
E
F
G
H
I
J
K
L
M
N
O
P
Q
R
S
T
U
V
W
X
Y
Z

177

look

I **look** far away.

M

mail

I got a letter in the **mail**.

many

There are **many** bees in the tree.

me

Kelly gave a snack to **me**.

meet

We **meet** nice people in our community.

moon

The **moon** is out at night.

music

A horn can make **music**.

my

I wear **my** new backpack to school.

178

N

neighborhood

I live in a **neighborhood**.

new

That hat is **new**.

O

of

I have a lot **of** friends.

one

Joe has **one** soccer ball.

open

The baby's mouth is **open**.

our

Our flag is on the moon.

out

Dave holds his hands **out**.

over

Can she go **over** the bar?

P

parade

They played in a **parade**.

A
B
C
D
E
F
G
H
I
J
K
L
M
N
O
P
Q
R
S
T
U
V
W
X
Y
Z

people

The **people** can smile.

play

We like to **play** football.

project

We worked on a **project**.

pumpkin

The **pumpkin** is round.

S

school

I like to go to **school**.

see

I **see** Ted.
Ted sees me.

she

She is a vet.

sleigh

The **sleigh** is on snow!

snack

This **snack** tastes good.

180

so

The turkey is **so** big.

soccer

I play **soccer**.

T

Thanksgiving

Thanksgiving is an American holiday.

the

The girl likes her drink.

then

I do my work. **Then** I go out to play.

they

They sort mail.

this

This letter is for Billy.

A B C D E F G H I J K L M N O P Q R **S T** U V W X Y Z

A
B
C
D
E
F
G
H
I
J
K
L
M
N
O
P
Q
R
S
T
U
V
W
X
Y
Z

three

I eat **three** times a day.

3

to

Stan likes **to** drum.

together

Max and Ray solve the problem **together**.

too

The hat is **too** big.

tortoise

A **tortoise** is slow.

two

There are **two** boys and **two** balls.

 U

use

Use a helmet to be safe!

 W

waddle

A duck can **waddle**.

wants

The duckling **wants** to come out of the egg.

182

water

Water is in a lake.

welcome

Welcome to our home!

where

Where do you live? Do you live in the United States?

white

The egg is **white**.

why

Why are the plants near the window?

with

We ate **with** each other.

work

The boys **work** together to fix the box.

worked

We **worked** hard in school.

world

I have friends all over the **world**.

Y

you

I show the book to **you**.

A B C D E F G H I J K L M N O P Q R S T U V W X Y Z

Index

Credits